You Are a Superhero, Too!

Brittnie Blackburn

WestBow Press books may be ordered through booksellers or by contacting:

WestBow Press
A Division of Thomas Nelson & Zondervan
1663 Liberty Drive
Bloomington, IN 47403
www.westbowpress.com
1 (866) 928-1240

Interior Image Credit: Siski Kalla

ISBN: 978-1-9736-9644-5 (sc)
ISBN: 978-1-9736-9645-2 (e)

Library of Congress Control Number: 2020912558

Print information available on the last page.

WestBow Press rev. date: 07/30/2020

WESTBOW
P R E S S®
A DIVISION OF THOMAS NELSON
& ZONDERVAN

Dedicated to my daughter, Camille.

You Are a Superhero, Too!

You, you, beautiful you. Did
you know, my dear, that
you are a superhero, too?

You sing, play, laugh, and make our days bright.
You love your sister with all of your might.

Your role is unique in this family of ours. You shine, little one, like the brightest of stars.

You, you, beautiful you. Did you know, my dear, that you are a superhero, too?

You continue to smile and give her
your heart, even when you wish
she played a different part.

You are a helper, a friend,
and her biggest fan. You are
always quick to shout, "Sister,
I know that you CAN!"

You, you, beautiful you. Did
you know, my dear, that
you are a superhero, too?

You explain to friends why your sister does not talk. You tell them she was two years old before she learned to walk.

You tag along to therapy and never get mad.
You would rather stay home, but never make her feel bad.

You, you, beautiful you. Did you know,
my dear, that you are a superhero, too?

You say it feels hard to watch brothers and sisters play.
Your sister will try, but then quickly walks away.

You cheer her on as she learns a new skill. You watch
her at mealtime to make sure she ate her fill.

You, you, beautiful you. Did you know, my dear, that you are a superhero, too?

You show kindness to all when
we must stop and meet her
need. You wait patiently and, at
times, even ask to take the lead.

You wish she ran
fast and played
hide-and-go-seek.
You wish she
danced with you
through puddles
and together
jumped a big leap.

You, you, beautiful you. Did you know, my
dear, that you are a superhero, too?

You gently take her hand
to walk outside to swing.
You share, "She has special
needs," when you sense
children being mean.

You wake everyday ready to offer your best. You show the world how we are all different but not less.

You, you, beautiful you. Did you know, my dear, that you are a superhero, too?

You join in her room as the
night sky grows dark. You
cuddle up and kiss her head
to leave your sister mark.

You say, "God made us all
different and that is okay!
Thank you, God, for my sister!
In your holy name I pray."

You, you, beautiful you. Did
you know, my dear, that
you are a superhero, too?

People call her a
superhero, and you
know it is true.

But you, my dear child,
are a superhero, too.

Printed in the United States
By Bookmasters